Life Beneath The Waves

Exploring the World of Ocean Animals

Miss Sierra

Siohan Press
www.siohanpress.com

Beneath the waves, the ocean thrives, A habitat where life survives.

From the surface to the deep,
Ecosystems never sleep.

Fish with scales and colors bright,
Swim through currents, left and right.

Adaptations keep them strong,
So in the ocean, they belong.

Crustaceans like crabs crawl low,
Using claws to grab and go.

The octopus, with arms so wide,
Changes shape and loves to hide.

Sea turtles glide through open seas, They migrate far with graceful ease.

Their journey long, from shore to shore,
To lay their eggs and swim once more.

Dolphins leap and hunt for prey,
Using echolocation in their play.

Jellyfish just float and glow,
With tentacles that drift below.

Sharks, the predators,
swim with grace,
Top of the food chain
in this place.

Whales, so mighty, sing their song,
In deep oceans, they belong.

The coral reef, a living thing,
A biodiverse home, where life can cling.

Symbiosis helps life grow,
Working together in the ocean flow.

The ocean's vast and full of wonder,
A system held in perfect order.

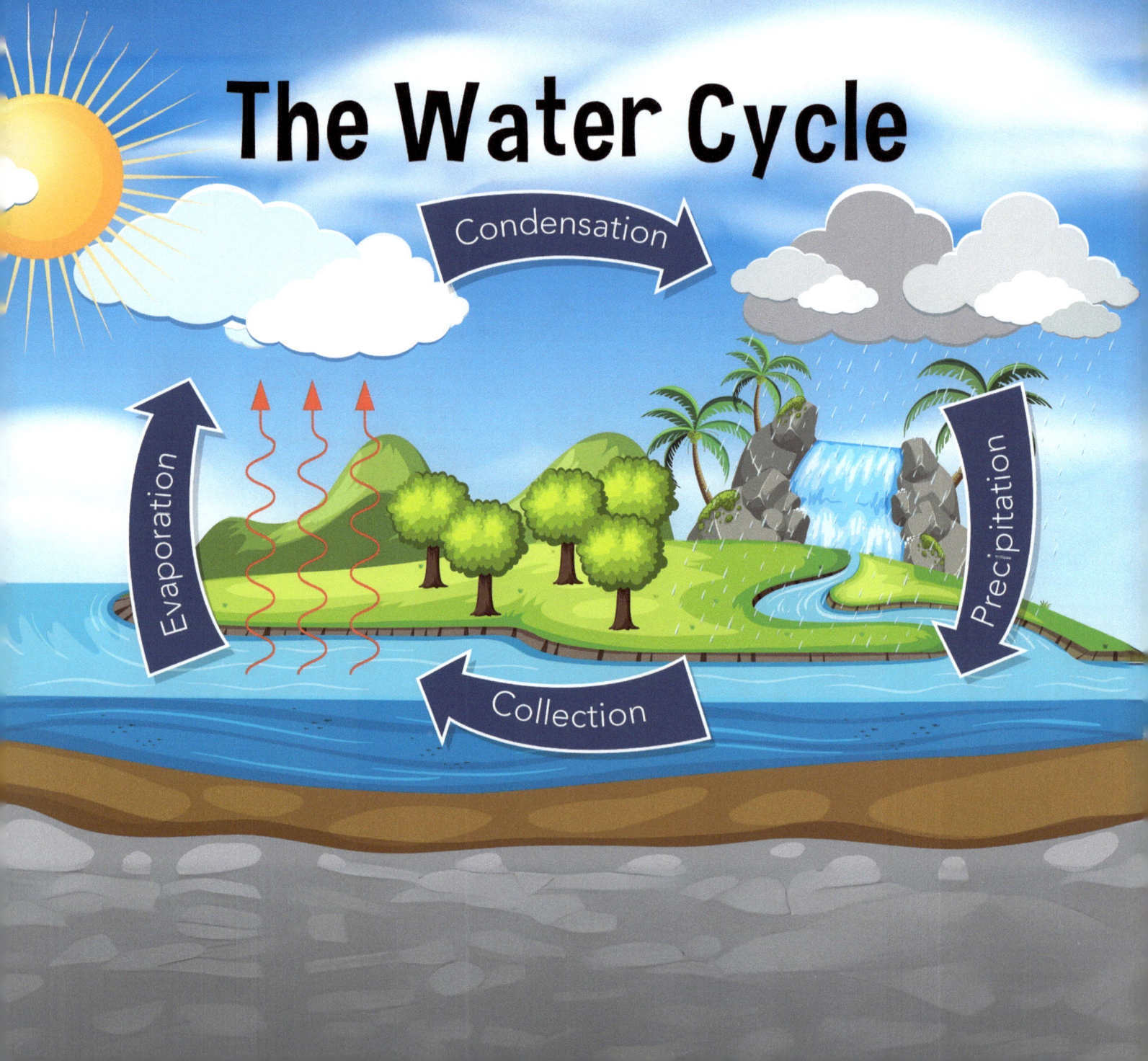

The Water Cycle

Condensation

Precipitation

Evaporation

Collection

It helps our world in many ways,
By balancing the climate's rays.

Vocabulary Words and Definitions

- **Ecosystem** – A community of living organisms, such as plants, animals, and microorganisms, that interact with each other and their physical environment, like the ocean or forest.
- **Adaptation** – A special feature or behavior that helps an animal or plant survive in its environment. For example, fish have gills to help them breathe underwater.
- **Crustacean** – A group of animals, like crabs, lobsters, and shrimp, that usually have a hard shell and live in water.
- **Echolocation** – A method used by animals, like dolphins and bats, to find objects by sending out sound waves that bounce back to them, helping them "see" with sound.

Vocabulary Words and Definitions

- **Migration** – The movement of animals from one place to another, often to find food or to reproduce. Sea turtles, for example, migrate long distances to lay their eggs.
- **Biodiversity** – The variety of life in a specific habitat, like a coral reef. More biodiversity means a healthier environment because different species help keep balance.
- **Symbiosis** – A relationship between two different species where both benefit from each other. For instance, some fish clean larger fish by eating parasites off their skin.
- **Predator** – An animal that hunts and eats other animals for food. Sharks are predators that play an important role in maintaining balance in the ocean's ecosystem.

YOUR COMMUNITY PARTNER
SiohanPress.com

SIOHAN PRESS
A PUBLISHING COMPANY

SCAN ME

Mailing List

Together we increase the confidence
and abilities of the children we love!

SIOHAN PRESS
A PUBLISHING COMPANY

Siohan Press LLC specializes in creating a diverse range of children's books designed to captivate young minds from Pre-K to 12th grade. Our extensive collection includes both fiction and non-fiction titles that cover a broad spectrum of topics, with a strong emphasis on STEM (Science, Technology, Engineering, and Mathematics) to inspire the next generation of innovators and problem-solvers.

Our engaging catalog features:

- **STEM Books**: Explore the wonders of science, technology, engineering, and mathematics through exciting stories and informative non-fiction that make complex concepts accessible and fun.

- **Fiction and Non-Fiction**: From imaginative tales that spark creativity to fact-filled books that satisfy curious minds, our selections are tailored to meet the diverse interests and educational needs of students at every grade level.

- **Coloring and Activity Books**: Foster creativity and fine motor skills with our beautifully illustrated coloring books and engaging activity books that provide hours of educational fun.

- **Guided Journals**: Encourage self-expression and reflective thinking with guided journals designed to help students articulate their thoughts and experiences.

- **Handwriting Practice Books**: Support foundational writing skills with our handwriting practice books, perfect for developing neat and confident writers.

Siohan Press LLC is dedicated to producing high-quality educational materials that not only meet but exceed the standards of school curriculums. Our books are meticulously crafted to engage students, enhance learning outcomes, and support educators in fostering a lifelong love of reading and learning.

Discover how Siohan Press LLC can be a valuable addition to your educational toolkit, providing students, parents, and families with the resources they need to succeed in an ever-evolving world. We look forward to your partnership.